Goldfish Suppers

An anthology of contemporary poems for children and families

Edited by Stewart Conn and Nancy Somerville

·EDINBVRGH·
THE CITY OF EDINBURGH COUNCIL

EDUCATION

Design and layout by David Gilchrist and Tracey Morrisey, Publications Unit, the City of Edinburgh Council Education Department

Front cover and title page illustrated by Aird McKinstrie

First published in 2004 by
The City of Edinburgh Council
Education Department
Wellington Court
10 Waterloo Place
Edinburgh EH1 3EG

The editors would like to acknowledge the support and assistance of the City of Edinburgh Council's Culture and Leisure Department in the planning of this book.

The publisher acknowledges subsidy from the Scottish Arts Council towards the publication of this volume.

ISBN 1 902299 36 1

Contents

Wee Blue Gnome

It's no easy
being wee
being a gnome

Yiv tae live unner mushrooms
an wear daft hats

Eat goldfish suppers – yiv
tae catch them yirsel

Dinnae get oot
till midnight – a quick
scamper across the lawn

Watch they dinnae SEE ye
watch they dinnae GET ye

Watch oot for that big dug

See me – see
when ah'm big

ah'm gaunny be
– ah UM!!! –
ah'm gaunny be
a
DRAGON!!!

Rawrrrr!

Billy Cornwall

Dookin Fur Aipples

dookin fur aipples
doon on yer hunkers
airms stuck ahint ye,
fork atween yer teeth,
drappin it
in
tae
jab yin aipple jigglin
in the bowl o watter,
joukin awa, dodgin
the fork -
but if ye couldnae spear't,
in wi yer face then,
dunk yer heid,
neb an a,
an grup yin
in yer teeth.

Angela B Brown
Illustrated by Moira Munro

Sound Bites

Back bacon, bran buds,
brown bread, big breakfast,
brunch.

Crisp crackers, crinkle crisps,
crusty croissants,
crunch.

Leafy lettuce, long leeks,
lollipops, luscious lemons,
lunch.

Marmalade, macaroni,
mussels, melon, mince,
munch.

Angela B Brown

Wee Poems
(four haiku)

baby duck so light
it *runs* across the leaves
of the waterlily

the child's red kite
surging, surging
against the wind

one small dog –
two hundred geese
panicked into flight

shrieks in the cold air –
a snowball fight
in the graveyard

Alan Spence
Illustrated by Moira Munro

from The Book of Why ...?

Why are birds alive?
Why do boats float?
Why are foals so little?
Why are there farmers?
Why was fruit invented?
Why do bats look so ugly?
Why do boys lark so much?
Why are all colds the same?
Why do radishes make my lips buzz?
Why do foxes live so deep in the woods?
Why do comets shoot through space at such tremendous speeds instead
of just floating?

Alec Finlay
Illustrated by Dave Sutton

Twinkle Twinkle Silver Star

Twinkle, twinkle, silver star,
Oh, I wonder what you are!
You look like a tasty treat,
Even good enough to eat,
In my mouth and down you went,
I thought you were from heaven sent.

Twinkle, twinkle, silver star,
Now I wonder where you are!
In my gullet you are stuck,
I think I've now run out of luck,
At hospital they'll have their say,
A price I'm going to have to pay.

Who're these men all dressed in green?
The likes before I've never seen,
I'm gently drifting far away,
But I'll live to see another day,
Feeling woozy, I'm coming round,
A silver star is what they found!

Anne Williamson

12

Mummy Says!

It's dinnertime again
Oh no! It's cabbage, peas and beans.
Mummy says as she waves her fork
"You've got to eat your greens!"

I'd rather have some ice cream
With sweeties on the top
But Mummy says "You eat too much
Your teeth are going to rot!"

Sometimes when I stay with Dad
We go into the town.
He takes me to the Burger Bar
And that makes Mummy frown.

"I've told you two before!" she says
"Junk food's bad for you!"
But Daddy told me afterwards
Mummy really loves burgers too!

Clare Duncan

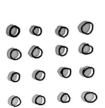

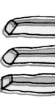

Dinner-Lady

Oor dinner-lady's a richt wee smasher
An if she's in a guid mood, ye get an extra rasher.

But get her oan a bad day, she's mingy wi the chips,
An it's strictly a "Nae Nonsense" day, her hans abune her hips.

She maks us scrumptious puddins, an mince an tatties too
An when she cries oot "Extras" ye should see us rin tae queue.

But when her horoscope's a scunner, an she's richt doon in the dumps
Watch oot fir frizzled sausages, an custard fu o lumps!

Margaret J Tollick
Illustrated by Dave Sutton

Penelope's Shoes

Penelope's shoes are blue with black buckles,
her wellington boots are shiny and red.
Her trainers are yellow with wavy white laces,
her slippers are tartan, they sit by her bed.

Penelope's shoes go visiting Granny,
her wellington boots go splash with a zoom.
Her trainers are running to keep up with Daddy,
her slippers are lonely and stay in her room.

Penelope's shoes are shopping in Asda,
her wellington boots can ride on a bus.
Her trainers are off to visit the Castle,
her slippers are shouting, "But what about us?"

Penelope's shoes feel yawny and sleepy,
her wellington boots are wet as can be.
Her trainers have tied themselves up in their laces,
her slippers are thinking, "It's time for the tea."

Penelope's Mum is calling, "It's bath time,"
she squeezes her sponge, she plays with her ships.
She puts on her nightie with lace at the collar,
then pops on her slippers and zoops up the zips.

Penelope's feet feel happy and comfy,
she whispers, "Hello, you're furry inside."
Penelope spins on her toes like a dancer,
her cosy warm slippers are bursting with pride.

Alma Shearer
Illustrated by Moira Munro

Try Again

There is a boy I know
Who does things by himself
He stands up on a chair
To reach the biscuit shelf

When he puts his clothes on
He really tries his best
His pants are back to front
And he can never find his vest

At dinnertime his plate's a mess
The ketchup's up the door
His chips are on the table
And his beans are on the floor

But when it comes to bedtime
He really is a gem
He goes to bed without a fuss
And in the morning…
Tries again!

Clare Duncan
Illustrated by Moira Munro

Aerial

Afloat on a sea of ice cream clouds,
I've a window seat, a god's eye view.

Everything's toy size: sheep in the field,
cars on the road, boats in the Firth,
a train crossing the rail bridge.
Bet I could pick it up, turn it around,
send it right back to Haymarket station.

I could fit all the boats in my bath,
cars under the bed, the sheep
in a shoebox, along with giraffes
from my zoo. And Arthur's Seat
is just a wee lump. I could jump it!

I spy The Castle and Holyrood Palace.
I'm trying to guess where my house is
when the pilot crackles across the tannoy:
Ladies and Gents, please fasten your seatbelts.
We're about to begin our descent.

Just after I've clunked and clicked
the plane coasts down like a swan,
the world on the ground gets closer
and bigger and bigger and Bmmff,
we're home! Bit of a bumpy landing.

Dilys Rose

A Little Nap Rap

When I got home one evening
to my cosy living room
I found a squirrel at my table
and a hedgehog with a broom.

A fox switched on the hoover,
beat my doormat with his tail,
while the squirrel did the kitchen
with a mophead and a pail.

The squirrel was all prickly
and the hedgehog had a tail,
the fox was dressed in tartan
while her coat hung on a nail.

The squirrel used the pulley
as trapeze, from side to side;
the fox slid down the banister,
the hedgehog did a glide.

My floor was very shiny
and everything was clean,
then suddenly I woke up
and found it was a dream!

Christine De Luca
Illustrated by Susan Scott

Daen It Again

I got a BMX bike fur ma birthday. It's braw
and I really wid like tae go ridin awa.
But she's got it, she has and she'll no gie it back.
She's been hoors gaun roon yon BMX track.
Demonstratin, she said, tae let me see hoo.
Weel, I'm fed up watchin and I waant a shot noo.
See, she's daen a wheelie and anither bunny hop,
a side kick and frame staun. She's never gaunae stop.
She's been ower they ramps that mony times,
peddlin sae quick ye'd hink she hud wings.
I've tried yellin an bawlin an greetin wi rage
but she waves back and roars 'Amin't I guid fur ma age?'
There's a crowd by the fence. They're cheerin hur oan.
They hink that bike's hers the wey she keeps gaun.
Ken, she's ay showin aff. I wish she hud her ain wan
cause I dinnae ken hoo tae git ma bike aff ma Gran.

Janet Paisley

Gorilla

Long arms, short legs,

Hairy back and knees,

Big eyes and wrinkly face,

Pot belly sure to please.

Big grin, strong jaws,

Happy face and looks,

Ensures that the gorilla finds

His place in poetry books.

Kendric Ross
Master of the Uni-verse

Football Fan

Here he comes – running through the station
After the match. Small boy, big yellow flag.

Watch him! He's a hero!
There's a lion dancing at his heels,
He's a hop, skip, whoop
Of hope
In all that might be possible
This game, next game,
This life, his.

Listen and you'll hear the lion
Roaring him on.

Diana Hendry
Illustrated by Keith Brumpton

Mary Had a Little Lamb

Mary had a little lamb,

potatoes and mint sauce –

onions fried in butter

and it made her ill because ………….

Mary ate too much of it,

she was an utter glutton,

she couldn't eat another bit

of chewy, gooey mutton.

Mary felt so very ill,

it really was a sin,

she had to call the doctor

who gave her me – … e – e … – eh dicine !

Kendric Ross
Master of the Uni-verse

Fireworks Aff the Castle

Fireworks aff the Castle
Goin WHEECH, WHEECH, WHEECH
Bairns in the library
Gettin WHEESHT, WHEESHT, WHEESHT

Cans o Irn Bru
Goin SKOOSHITAY, SKOOSHITAY, SKOOSH
Fitbaw in the playgroond
Gettin DOOSHITAY, DOOSHITAY, DOOSH

The snaw blaws in fae Norroway
And nips your TAES, TAES, TAES
We go skitin on wir sledges
Doon the BRAES, BRAES, BRAES

The rain comes doon in buckets
And it's WEET, WEET, WEET
Your teeth is sair fae sweeties
And it's GREET, GREET, GREET

You're oot wi pals and aw the time
It's BLETHER, BLETHER, BLETHER
But when awthin's wrang and no goin right
Jist go and tell your MITHER
When awthin's wrang and no goin right
Jist you coorie in wi MITHER

Matthew Fitt
Illustrated by Moira Munro

Duddingston, Blackford and Portobello

Down by the loch,
I saw a goose
Gobbling and gabbling

Down by the pond
I saw a duck
Ducking and diving

Down by the sea
I saw a gull
Swooping and screeching

Now I'm home
I'm keeping my crumbs
To give to the goose, gobbling and gabbling
To drop for the duck, ducking and diving
To throw high in the air for the gull swooping and screeching.

Hatty Chick
Illustrated by Alexa Rutherford

Crisps an Cola

Allie-ballie, Allie-ballie-bee
Sittin on yir Mammie's knee
Greetin fir a fifty-p
Tae buy some crisps an cola.

Ma wee Jeannie's roon's a butter-ba
A hir claes ir far too sma
The doctor says it'll nivir dae at a
Tae gie her crisps an cola.

Allie-ballie, Allie-ballie-bee
Sittin on yir Mammie's knee
Greetin fir a fifty-p
Tae buy some crisps an cola.

Margaret J Tollick

Riches

In my language everybody says

Grandchildren are the interest

On your investment

My son was my investment in life

You my sweet granddaughter are my interest

The bonus comes in your hugs and kisses

Your first words were like gold coins.

Rasida Patel

The Ogley Mogley Man

It's dead of night in my bedroom
It's black as hell: no stars or moon
I hear evil sounds
deep down underground
Here comes the Ogley Mogley Man

His teeth are green; his nose is blue
His eyes are red and yellow too
I'm not really scared
but that's him on the stairs
Here comes the Ogley Mogley Man

On every step I hear his tread
It's time to hide beneath the bed
I mustn't make a sound
He's on the landing now
Here comes the Ogley Mogley Man ...

I hear the door creak open wide
There's one low growl and he's inside
Creeping to my bed
He wants to kill me dead
Here comes the Ogley Mogley Man

He grabs the quilt and starts to swear
He's not got me, just my teddy-bear
I laugh and scramble out
Kick his bum, scream and shout
JOBBIES, OGLEY MOGLEY MAN!

I stare into his yellow eye
He backs away and starts to cry
He runs away so frit and scared
He trips and falls down all the stairs
There goes the Ogley Mogley Man

Mike Dillon
Illustrated by Keith Brumpton

Sailing to Mousa Broch

On holiday in Shetland

On a little boat

Sailing to Mousa Broch

And the only thing I want to do

Is lick the side of the boat

The saltiest, tastiest taste I've ever tasted

But I can't let mum and dad see

Because they'll say it's dirty

And tell me to stop

But if they licked it too

Then they'd know

And we could lick the boat together

All the way to Mousa

Stephen Barnaby

A 50 Word Poem about Cats Taking Over My School

One day
cats took over my school
and that was good
because they sat on all the books and jotters
and fell asleep
and we didn't have to do any work

There was just one problem

for some reason
we stopped getting our daily pint of milk

I wonder why?

Stephen Barnaby
Illustrated by Susan Scott

What No One Can Know

Look in the mirror, breathe on the glass,
there you will see what must come to pass.
Are you a smile, a laugh or a frown?
Will you grow up, or will you grow down?

At night when you sleep, the world is your own:
no sunlight or moonlight – *your* light alone.
What do you see when you close your eyes?
– for this is a darkness that cannot tell lies.

Where have you come from? Where will you go?
These are unknowns that no one can know.
But sometimes a moment will come when it seems
you *know* who you are, and the rest is all dreams.

And when it does, then don't turn away,
don't be afraid to stand up and say:
'I am who I am, and know I am free
to be who I will: and I will be ME!'

Ron Butlin
Illustrated by Alexa Rutherford

About the Contributors

EDITORS

Stewart Conn, who lives in Edinburgh, is currently the capital's Makar (or poet laureate), and honorary president of Shore Poets. www.shorepoets.org.uk

Nancy Somerville coordinates Edinburgh's team of Family Learning Workers. She is a published poet and a member of Shore Poets.

POETS

Stephen Barnaby was raised by stoats and left able to communicate only in fifty squeaky noises, translated especially for this anthology.

Angela B Brown taught languages. She combines work in the Scottish Poetry Library with M Phil studies in Creative Writing at Glasgow University.

Ron Butlin's work has won several Scottish Arts Council Book Awards. Two new story collections *Vivaldi and The Number 3* and *No More Angels* will appear in summer 2004. He lives in Edinburgh.

Hatty Chick has lived in Edinburgh since 1984. She works as an Educational Psychologist with the City of Edinburgh.

Billy Cornwall was born in Leith and brung up in various parts of Edinburgh – a neat trick! His daftish poems and more serious stories have appeared in magazines as diverse as *Scottish Child, Rebel Inc* and *Cencrastus*.

Christine De Luca writes in both English and Shetlandic. She has published three collections, and made many contributions to anthologies, mixed media exhibitions and poetry events. She is a member of Shore Poets.

Mike Dillon, singer/songwriter and poet, lives in Edinburgh. He has published two poetry collections and recently released a CD of his songs.

Clare Duncan is a thirty-something single mum, living in the Moredun area of Edinburgh with her young son.

Alec Finlay (born in Inverness in 1966) is an artist, poet and publisher (Morning Star, pocketbooks & platform). He is currently artist in residence at Westlea Primary School (Seaham), where he is collecting questions asked by kids aged 3–5 years for *The Book of Questions*, and working with Amparo Montero Espina (aged 8 years) from Uruguay, collecting photographs of everyone's eyes.

Matthew Fitt was born in Dundee and has been stottin aboot all over the shop ever since. He now lives near Edinburgh in a wee cottage with three lums, a big gairden and with a burn running alongside it.

Diana Hendry is a poet, novelist and writer for children. Her latest book is *No Homework Tomorrow* (published by Glowworm). She lives in Edinburgh and is a member of Shore Poets.

Janet Paisley is an award-winning poet, author, playwright, non-fiction, script and screenwriter, who writes in Scots and English.

Rasida Patel likes to write poetry at the CLAN Pins and Pens Group at Shakti Women's Aid. Shakti have been like a family to Rasida since 1998.

Dilys Rose lives in Edinburgh with her family and a cat called Jeep. She also writes for grown-ups. Further information: www.dilysrose.com

Kendric Ross is author of *Classic Children's Games from Scotland*, and Scotland's number one Nonsense Poet – even funnier than Mike Spilligan?

Alma Shearer has one daughter and three grandchildren who play a significant part in her everyday life. She is a keen singer, loves writing for young people and is deeply interested in all wildlife. Last but not least, she's a Harry Potter addict.

Alan Spence is a poet and playwright, novelist and short story writer. He is also Professor in Creative Writing at the University of Aberdeen.

Margaret Tollick is an active member of the Scottish Storytelling Forum. She has had other poems published in *My Mum's a Punk* (Scottish Children's Press) and *King o the Midden* (Itchy Coo Publishing).

Anne Williamson, an Edinburgh lass, is married with two sons, enjoys writing poems/ rhymes, usually after times of sleep deprivation and stress.

ILLUSTRATORS

Keith Brumpton, creator of countless characters, books and terrible puns, began drawing at primary school. Now Glasgow-based, he writes (and draws) for TV, film and theatre as well as for books like this.

Keith Brumpton
Flat 2/1
50 Kelvin Drive
GLASGOW
G20 8QN
Tel: 0141 945 4812
Fax: 0141 945 4812
Email: keith.brumpton@virgin.net
www.keithbrumpton.co.uk

Aird McKinstrie,
Born in 56 in equatorial swelter –
Port Harcourt on the Niger Delta.
Education varied, never thorough,
Completed school in Edinburgh.
Art School – Gray's in Aberdeen,
Staff tolerant but hardly keen.
Illustration has maintained sanity,
Worldwide clients help his vanity.

Aird McKinstrie
McKinstrie Wilde
62 Newhaven Road
EDINBURGH
EH6 5QB
Tel: 0131 554 4441
Fax: 0131 554 9496
Email: aird@mckinstriewilde.co.uk

Moira Munro, writer and illustrator of children's books, also draws cartoons for grown-up publications. Her school visits whip up enthusiasm in children and teachers alike. Whatever your age, check out www.moiramunro.com

Moira Munro
69 Lomondside Avenue
GLASGOW
G76 7UH
Tel: 0141 638 9851
Email: moira@moiramunro.com

Alexa Rutherford studied illustration at Duncan of Jordanstone, Dundee. She is now based in Edinburgh working freelance, mainly for publishers in the UK and USA.

Alexa Rutherford
64 Grange Loan
EDINBURGH
EH9 2EP
Tel: 0131 667 2443
Fax: 0131 667 2443
Email: alexarutherford@aol.com
www.alexarutherford.co.uk

Susan Scott, born in Glasgow in 1962, drew pictures before she could walk. She graduated from Glasgow School of Art in 1984 and has been illustrating ever since!

Susan Scott
Flat 2/1
12 Yorkhill Street
GLASGOW
G3 8SB
Tel: 0141 339 5170
Fax: 0141 339 5170
Email: susan.scott4@btinternet.com

Dave Sutton can be spotted wandering Edinburgh with a sketchbook glued to his hands (when he's not scuba-diving or playing tennis).

Dave Sutton
7 St Peter's Buildings
Gilmore Place
EDINBURGH
EH3 9PG
Tel: 0131 228 3375
Email: d.sutton@virgin.net or dave@suttonstuff.com

You will find more illustrations at www.scottishillustrators.com

About Family Learning

The Family Learning Service in Edinburgh offers programmes of activities to enable parents/carers of pre-school and lower primary aged children to support their children's literacy and numeracy through the development of their own learning. Family Learning groups meet in primary schools, nurseries and other community settings in various areas of the city.

For more information, please contact:

Nancy Somerville
Community Education Headquarters
Wellington Court
10 Waterloo Place
EDINBURGH
EH1 3EG
Telephone: 0131 200 2000 ext 4002
Email: nancy.somerville@educ.edin.gov.uk